# MAHLER

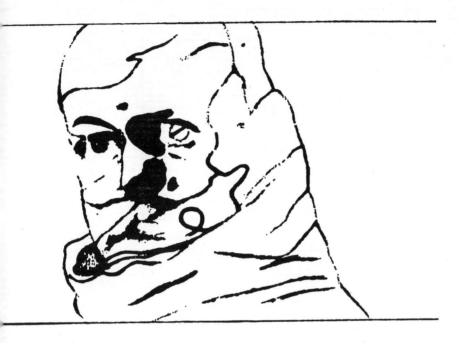

*JONATHAN WILLIAMS*

# MAHLER

CAPE GOLIARD PRESS
IN ASSOCIATION WITH
GROSSMAN PUBLISHERS NEW YORK

*for Tom Meyer*

# A NOTE FOR THE FIRST EDITION

*"My time has not yet come, but your time is always ready."*
—Mahler

It would seem, finally, that *response* is the most necessary function
for us—as men and as artists. I find it put exactly by Robert Duncan's
lines from the poem, "The Law I Love Is Major Mover":

> *Responsibility is to keep*
> *the ability to respond.*

Since I first heard a performance of Gustav Mahler's *Symphony
No. 1, in D Major* by the Philadelphia Orchestra under Eugene
Ormandy on November 8, 1949 in Carnegie Hall, New York, I have
been more responsive to his music than to any other. In other words,
for some fifteen years now. And so it seems fitting, in May 1964,
when the Yellow-Billed Cuckoo has returned to these mountains
and intimately evokes the First Symphony, to practice these exercises
in spontaneous composition to the movements of all the Mahler
symphonies. I am interested in gauging my response in compositions
of language to the sounds of the music, not in imitating the sounds,
which would be futile and silly. My desire to make this homage to
Mahler is well expressed by the critic Paul Stefan in his book,
*Gustav Mahler: A Study of His Personality and Work* (G. Schirmer,
New York, 1913). Stefan is quoting Schopenhauer as his principal
witness: "Our age . . . sees in this life (the sluggish blood of the
Too-Many never yet succeeded in attaining to *life*) only sin and
lamentation, hurry and restlessness. At best it seeks hastily and
superficially to conform itself to it, oftenest in the end condemning
it as superficial. And therefore our 'men of culture,' those who
'acknowledge' our time, 'make an end as quickly as possible of
everything, works of art, beautiful natural objects, and the really
valuable view of life in all its scenes.' "

In his very useful insights, Stefan says at another point: "In general,
the hearer who interprets rather than listens likes nothing better than
to investigate what the composer 'meant' by his works. Of course, he
meant nothing whatever. But by means of a symbol, an image, one
may better understand his works. Beethoven's headings and
instructions and Schumann's titles are intended to be thus understood,
and in this sense Mahler's symphonies can here and there be
described in words; often the words of the vocal movements

themselves invite it . . . " He mentions for instance the programme that Mahler attached to early performances of the First Symphony in Hamburg and Weimar: "Part I. The Days of Youth. Youth, flowers and thorns. (1) Spring without end. The introduction represents the awakening of nature at early dawn. (Nota: in Hamburg it was called 'Winter Sleep.') (2) A Chapter of Flowers (Andante). (3) Full Sail (Scherzo)," and so on. He then quotes the young Bruno Walter: "Let us be prudent enough to free these titles from an exact meaning, and remember in the kingdom of beauty nothing is to be found except '*Gestaltung, Umgestaltung, des ewigen Sinnes ewige Unterhaltung.*' (Formation, Transformation, the Eternal Mind's Eternal Recreation.) . . . We must not think of that 'which the flowers of the meadow tell,' but of everything that touches our hearts with gentlest beauty and tenderest charm."

So, then, these responses to the music. They were written *only* during the duration of each movement, lest the com-posing get too elaborated. The titles are simply the musical markings of the movements, in my amateur translations. I have used earphones to listen to the recordings in my collection, which serve to blot out extraneous background noise and enhance the concentration. Another useful exercise might be to draw with the eyes shut, using only the motor faculty while listening with closest attention. This is a technique we employed at Moholy-Nagy's Institute of Design in Chicago to 'liberate' response.

Finally, while the poems are spontaneous and reworked once or twice at the most (during a second performance of a movement), the background for writing them is not random. I am calling upon fifteen years of performances, recordings, and readings. Of the First Symphony, I am fortunate to have heard it in person by Ormandy, Walter, Kubelik, Barbirolli, and Mitropoulos; and on records also by Kletzki, Leinsdorf, Boult, Horenstein, Scherchen, and Steinberg. The books I have are by Alma Mahler, Dika Newlin, Schoenberg, Krenek, Guido Adler, Paul Stefan, Richard Specht, and Bruno Walter. I regret that I cannot read the collection of Mahler's own letters (1879-1911), not available yet (I think) in English. My other information is everything else I know and am moved by. To end with Paul Stefan: "The music, dewy fresh, strikes the goggles from the nose of the peering critic."

*Jonathan Williams*
*Highlands, North Carolina*
*May—June 1964*

# A NOTE FOR THE PRESENT EDITION

R. B. Kitaj, the old Chagrin Falls Flash and Tracer of Lost Persons, picked up the poems and ran with them. Quoting his "Mahler: A Celebration and a Crutch" (in the exhibition catalogue of the Marlborough-Gerson Gallery, New York, February, 1965): "Jonathan Williams has written 40 poems responding to Mahler's symphonies and I have begun (Fall 1964) to make a run of prints using the music, the poems, the Mahler literature and times and a good deal else as a compound crutch upon which to hang much that cannot be made to splice easily with Mahler. In this light Mahler's own ambiguous, lifelong attitude towards 'The vexed problem of programme music' is worth noting and he reminds us that 'The creative urge for a musical organism certainly springs from an experience of its author, i.e., from a fact, after all, which should be positive enough to be expressible in words . . .' and also that 'My music arrives at a programme as its last clarification, whereas in the case of Richard Strauss the programme already exists as a given task . . .'

"Thanks are due to H. R. Fischer for his encouragement of the work at hand which will often spring from music which he knows in ways I never will and to Chris Prater, who is printing the work . . . much of the essence of the thing is in his hands. We hope to bring out the prints one day in an edition of 50 on various papers with the Williams sequence in the place of honour . . ."

*Marlborough Fine Art Limited*, London did in fact publish the suite of screen prints (15 in number) together with a book of the original 40 poems. Printed by Tillotsons; designed by Gordon House; 30 copies in commerce, numbered and signed by the poet; issued in the summer of 1967.

For the present edition by *Cape Goliard Press Limited*, Kitaj has kindly prepared special covers, in lieu of the screen prints which would cost you about 400 guineas. The sinister portrait of the poet on the title page is from Kitaj's painting, "Aureolin" (1964), of Col. J. Williams (Musical Director of the Macon County North Carolina Meshuga Sound Society).

Minor adjustments, clarifications, and (hopefully) improvements have been made on the poems of symphonies I through 9. The *Tenth Symphony* is new. When I wrote the others in the spring of 1964 I did not have available a recording of Dercyk Cooke's 'performing version' of the symphony with the five movements complete. Eugene Ormandy's performance of this score on Columbia is a very fine one, and he and Mr. Cooke, particularly, deserve our thanks. The one movement, the *Adagio*, I knew from the *Tenth* is now re-written and joined by the rest of the work. I would like to put on the earphones again in about ten years and see what Mahler has to tell me. The message appears to be coming in louder and clearer, what with this Christmas's package of nine symphonies and *Das Lied* by Bernstein; and the likelihood of similar collections from DGG and Victor within another year or two. I hope not to be put off by these astonishing populist developments and chased back into the arcanum of the 90-year-old gent who wrote the *Universe Symphony*, or the *Turangalila* of Messiaen, or Goldmark, or Schrecker, or Medtner, or Kurt Atterburg, who finished the Unfinished Symphony. I think not. As a matter of fact I am conducting an investigation into the number of cuckoos in the *First Symphony* of Mahler—mimetic or purely musical intervals. Dr. Herbert Brün is my accomplice, and the results will show when I next sit down to write my findings, perhaps in March 1979 in the West Riding of York.

*Jonathan Williams*
*Aspen Institute for Humanistic Studies*
Aspen, Colorado 81611
December 8, 1967

# SYMPHONY No. 1, IN D MAJOR

" . . . to write a symphony means, to me, to
construct a world with all the tools of
the available technique. The ever-new and
changing content determines its own form."
—Mahler, 1895

I. *Slowly—dragging, like a sound of nature*

Moravian plains . . . dawn . . . horns and bassoons down below
dawn . . .

o hello, cuckoos,
hello, bluebells and bugles
in a spring rain

Orpheus strings the wind with the mind's
terrains

kling! kling!

o yes, Linnaeus,
"the marsh marigold blows when the cuckoo sings!"

and the sunshine
sings

and the sunshine sings
all things

open

## II. *Strongly agitated, but not too fast*

it's doubtful whether
rustic Austrian bees,
as described by Professor Von Frisch,
dance round
sunny boxwoods so
stately, so ceremoniously as
this

but, brown thrashers in dirt, chirping 3/4 time—
yes

III. *Solemn and measured, without dragging*

two blue eyes
too blew ayes
to loose ice . . .

        merrily down the
        merrily verily merrily verily
        down the stream

        where *la vida*
        *es sueño* is

        a dream
        down the stream
        under the *linden*
        *baum*

ice, yes, eyes
streamed

IV. *Stormily agitated*

the things seen, the
intervals, and the noises
are nature's, Dr.
Williams:

"Measure serves for us as the key:
we can measure between objects;
therefore we know that they
exist."


lichens on aspens
seen in green
lightning


the crack of perception isn't too quick,
the cuckoo's call is tuned by
adrenalin glands,
clouds linked to the world
by lightning and tuning—it cracks the
stones and melts the heart

the cuckoo takes heart, eye-bright
in blue air, lightning

hits it

# SYMPHONY No. 2, IN C MINOR

> *What is the answer?*
> *What was the question?*
> —Gertrude Stein (last words)

I. *"Pompes Funèbres": briskly, majestically, with complete gravity & solemnity of expression*

"why live, why
suffer?

because of a
great joke, an
absurd joke?

we ask these old
questions, to

continue to live
to continue
dying . . ."

an empyrean hand
touching the
stem of
a great gold sunflower

in absolute
silence

a farina of seeds filling
the sky

in absolute
silence

## II. *Moderately slow: "Schubertian"*

sun
on
rain
clouds

summer sun
on
ploughed
clods

paeans of
loud
sunshine

III. *"St. Anthony of Padua's Sermon to the Fishes"*:
*in a quiet, flowing motion*


Padua's Anthony's
ichthyo-euphony—
yeah! yeah! yeah!

sermon's over,
fish same as ever—
blah! blah! blah!

stupidity today!
moribundity tomorrow!
rah! rah! rah!

IV. *"Primeval Light" : very solemn, but simple*


"in an artist
it must come from
a sense of totality; the whole;
and humanity as a whole.
How can a man be satisfied
when he sees another man
lacking——"


I am from God, and
must to God return


While we slept these kept with us:
the grosbeak's breast in the early sun,
the wood thrush's notes, ants
in the leaves,
mallows in the wind and
dogwoods opening


the world of the little hears little Mahler,
but while we slept
these kept with us

V. *Scherzo tempo. all stops out*


The Lord of Orchards
selects his fruits
in the Firmament's
breast.

'Hogs live in the present;
Poets live in the past,''
said Palmer. Orchards are
where the air
is blessed.

# SYMPHONY No. 3, IN D MINOR

*"Thousands lavishing, thousands starving;*
*intrigues, wars, flatteries, envyings,*
*hypocrisies, lying vanities, hollow amusements,*
*exhaustion, dissipation, death—and giddiness*
*and laughter, from the first scene to the*
*last."*

—Samuel Palmer, 1858

## I. *Pan Awakes: Summer Marches In*

Pan's
spring rain
"drives his victims
out to the animals
with whom they become
as one"—


pain and paeans,
hung in the mouth,

to be sung

## II. *What the Flowers in the Meadow Tell Me*

June 6, 1857, Thoreau in his *Journal:*

*A year is made up of a certain series*
*and number of sensations and thoughts*
*which have their language in nature . . .*

*Now I am ice, now*
*I am sorrel.*

Or, Clare, 1840, Epping Forest:

*I found the poems in the fields*
*And only wrote them down*

and

*The book I love is everywhere*
*And not in idle words*

John, *claritas* tells us the words are *not* idle,
the syllables are able
to turn plantains into quatrains,
tune *raceme* to *cyme, panicle* and *umbel* to
form corollas in light clusters of tones . . .

Sam Palmer hit it:
"Milton, by one epithet
draws an oak of the largest girth I ever saw,
'Pine and *monumental* oak':
I have just been trying to draw a large one in
Lullingstone; but the poet's tree is huger than
any in the park."

Muse in a meadow, compose in
a mind!

III. *What the Animals in the Forest Tell Me*


Harris's Sparrow—

103 species seen
by the Georgia Ornithological Society
in Rabun Gap,

including Harris's Sparrow, with its
black crown, face, and bib encircling
a pink bill


It was, I think, the third sighting
in Georgia, and I should have been there
instead of reading Clare, listening to
catbirds and worrying about
*turdus migratorius* that flew
directly into the Volkswagen and
bounced into a ditch


Friend Robin, I cannot figure it, if I'd
been going 40 you might be
whistling in some grass.

10 tepid people got 10 stale letters
one day earlier,
I cannot be happy
about that.

IV. *What the Night Tells Me*


the dark drones on
in the southern wheat fields
and the hop flowers
open before the sun's
beckoning


the end
is ripeness, the wind
rises,
and the dawn says
yes


YES! it says
"yes"

## V. *What the Morning Bells Tell Me*

*Sounds, and sweet aires*
*that give delight*
*and hurt not—*

that, let
Shakespeare's
delectation
bear us

## VI. *What Love Tells Me*

Anton Bruckner counts the 877th leaf
on a linden tree in the countryside near Wien
and prays:

Dear God, Sweet Jesus,
Save Us, Save Us . . .

the Light in the Grass,
the Wind on the Hill,

are in my head,
the world cannot be heard

Leaves obliterate
my heart,

we touch each other
far apart . . .

Let us count
into
the Darkness

# SYMPHONY No. 4, IN G MAJOR

> " . . . *inter urinas et faeces nascimur.*"
> —St. Augustine

I. *Serene—wary, not hurried*

" Happinesses have wings and wheels;
miseries are leaden legged;
and their whole employment is to clip
the wings and take off the wheels
of our chariots.
We determine, therefore, to be happy
and do all that we can, tho' not
all that we would,"

said William Blake in Felpham, Sussex

And so there are
mysterious chariots chanting
charivaris and planting
*haricots verts*
in the air
over Thomas Hariot's Cheviot
potato patch

Everything should be
as simple as
it is,
but *not*
simpler,
agreed Professor
Einstein, a stone's throw
away in Chariot

Eight

II. *In a comfortable motion*

"*like a fiend in a cloud,*"
Death calls the tune,
plays out of tune and arrives
in a cloud

heard only by the catbird,
who sits in Death's June sunshine
and sings the tune again

and again

and simply continues singing:

*black eye/blue sky!*
*black eye/blue sky!*

III. *Restful*

"I live in a hole here,
but God has a beautiful mansion for me elsewhere."

O grow
a Mountain in Fountain
Court

Sundown over
London

Kate Blake
in black

IV. *Very comfortably*


St. Peter looks on in Heaven,
6 O'clock, Sunday, the 12th of August 1827:

"Lest you should not have heard
of the Death of Mr. Blake
I have written this to inform you . . .

—Just before he died His Countenance became fair—
His eyes Brighten'd and He burst out in Singing
of the things he Saw in Heaven. In truth He Died
like a Saint as a Person who was standing by Him
Observed . . ."


No music on earth
is there
that might ever compare
with ours

# SYMPHONY No. 5, IN C SHARP MINOR

*"How blessed, how blessed a tailor to be!*
*Oh that I had been born a commercial traveller*
*and engaged as baritone at the Opera! Oh that*
*I might give my Symphony its first performance*
*fifty years after my death!"*

—Mahler, 1904

I. *Funeral March*

Mahler, from his studio on the eleventh floor of the
Hotel Majestic, New York City, hears the cortege of a
fireman moving up Central Park West:

one roll of the drum

one road where the wind storms, where
Cherubim sing birds' songs
with human faces and hold the world
in human hands and
drift on the gold road
where black wheels smash
all

one roll of the drum

II. *Stormily agitated*

to be a block of flowers
in a wood

to be mindlessly in flower
past understanding

to be shone on
endlessly

to be *there*, there
and blessed

III. *Scherzo*

one two three
one two three

little birds waltz to and fro
in the piano

at Maiernigg on the
Wörthersee

and up the tree:
cacophony

one two three

IV. *Adagietto*

one feels
one clematis petal
fell

its circle
is all

glimmer on this pale
river

V. *Rondo-Finale*


Schoenberg: "I should
even have liked to observe
how Mahler
knotted his tie,

and should have found that
more interesting and instructive
than learning how
one of our musical bigwigs composes
on a 'sacred subject.'

. . . An apostle
who does not glow
preaches heresy."


his tie was knotted
with éclat
on
the dead run!

# SYMPHONY No. 6, IN A MINOR

*"The life and knowledge of God may doubtless
be described as love playing with itself;
but this idea sinks into triviality, if the
seriousness, the pain, the patience and the
labor of the Negative are omitted."*

—Hegel

I. *Brisk, with energy, but not too much*

O Alma, Almschili, Almaschel, Almschi, Almscherl—

the dream
does not know
the word
'no'

Alma Mahler

*O Alma! Mater! O Cybele!*
*Jubilate!*

## II. *Moderately slow*

"When we're alone for a time we achieve
a unity with ourselves and nature . . .

we become positive
(instead of stuck in negation)
and finally productive

the commonplace takes us farther and farther
from ourselves
but we are brought back to ourselves
by solitude,
and from ourselves to God
is only a step.

Yes, I am lost to the world
with which I used to waste much time.

I live alone in my heaven,
In my love, in my song."


the cowbells
on the hills

are far
below

## III. *Scherzo*

one potato two potato
three potato four

so, off the floor
out the door

to grandfather's
flowers
by the lake-
shore

little girl, that man
is Frankenstein, not your
grandfather


one potato two potato
three potato four,

Mr?

## IV. *Finale*

It is the *hero*
on whom fall
three blows of fate,

the last of which
fells him
as a tree is
felled.


" He was a tree
in full leaf
and flower."

# SYMPHONY No. 7, IN B MINOR

*"The poet, no less than the scientist,
works on the assumption that inert and
live things and relations hold enough
interest to keep him alive as part of
nature."*

—Louis Zukofsky

I. *Adagio*

dark green radiance
beast snarl
yellow shadow

lucidity, touch,
blood, pulse

.

moon black empyrean fire,
awe,
stone cascade

body, eye, birth,
laugh

II. *Night Music, moderately fast*

the halcyon sun
opens
and captures
night's raging epiphanies

hands love
in a cool wood

.

poems and paeans
move time
in celebrations

the blue bird
dreams
of hot, coiling play

III. *Like a shadow*

hair
ear

globe
roar

flesh
flash

white
song

spectrum

life
mystery

.

mouth
smile

pleasure
dance

wind
tracery

energy
yield

pool

shining
image

IV. *Night Music, slowly, lovingly*

melodies whir,
muscles glory,

the locale lights,
red embraces,

and ecology
mixes April

.

tones breathe,
touch charges,

and justice circuits:

once blooming leaves water October earth

## V. *Rondo-Finale*

Blake's Mission:

a Flowering Heart,
Delight in the Lungs,

Calm Trance,

a gold cloud
at gloaming

.

Mahler's Vision:

Eternal Atonement,
Music's Exuberance,

Air & Waterfalls

Come, Death-Spirit!

*Note:* Following the lead of Louis Zukofsky's inscription on the viability of the relationships for the poet between 'inert and live things,' I have made the poems of the *Symphony No. 7, in B Minor* through the use of an 'Hallucinatory Deck.' This is a personal, alchemical deck of 55 white cards on which are written 110 words—the private and most meaningful words of my poetic vocabulary. One then plays with the deck in various ways. In this case, I dealt out 11 cards for each of the five movements of the symphony. In the first movement they are combined but left as simple nouns, verbs, and adjectives. In the second movement, particles have been added and a simple connecting syntax. In the third movement the deal is left as it fell from the deck—each 11 cards having 22 words. In the fourth movement, nouns are made to act with verbs. The fifth movement yields a very extraordinary constellation and is the most hallucinatory of the five deals. Around the words *Blake* and *Mahler* the dealer was given a chain of precise meanings which more than justified the use of the deck in the experiment . . . My knowledge of the deck derives from the poet Michael McClure, who credits the Los Angeles painter George Herms with its invention.

J.W.

# SYMPHONY No. 8, IN E FLAT MAJOR

*"Nature swells from herring to leviathan,*
*from the hodmandod to the elephant, so,*
*divine Art piles mountains on her hills,*
*and continents upon those mountains."*
—Samuel Palmer, 1828

I. *Hymn: "Veni, Creator Spiritus!"*

Since—since—since Brahms,
nothing has been written equal it,
gasped an eccentric American.

Spitting on the floor
does not help you to be Beethoven,
snapped Mahler.

II. *Closing Scene from Goethe's "Faust"*


all that is transitory
is but an image


a world presented
and fashioned step by step—

it will be *actual*,
there will be no paraphrase,
no similitudes and images . . .


what *actual* need is there of notes?
"I can only say it once more by means of an image":

hemerocallis is
a Goddess's dark orange chalice,
in the blue beyond
the blessed clouds


God (Gustav Mahler) looked
and saw that it was good.

Eros is Creator
of the World.

SYMPHONY No. 9, IN D

1. *Moderately slow*

what will you do, God,
when I am dead?

not quote
Rilke

II. *In the time of an easy Austrian Landler*


We'll go to Egypt and see nothing but blue sky,
we'll walk across water on my matted streptococci—

that will be the day
to be happy


systole, diastole, dance
the holy dance!

## III. *Rondo: Burleske*

what's red, bleeds—
and runs in circles?

the miracle
of the art of
the human
heart

in a sweat

IV. *Adagio*

Grinzing cemetery, outside Wien, May 19, 1911:

the sun shone on
on one alone


*"Bless* relaxes"

# SYMPHONY No. 10, IN F SHARP MINOR

*"Grace is courage to try to put the world
in order through love."*

—Hildegard Jone

Yea, Lord!

cowbells, cold streams, warm hills, animals
die, we

die . . . *"ewig, ewig"* . . . *Das Lied
Von Der Erde*

red red red *Der
Erde*

Anton Webern's last words were
*es ist aus*

Hans Moldenhauer's
book on the death
tells us about Raymond N. Bell,
American Army cook,
who fired three shots the night of September 15, 1945
and killed Webern:

*Mount Olive, North Carolina
April 7, 1960*

*" . . . My husband's middle name was Norwood. Date of birth was
August 16, 1914. We have one son who will be 21 in June. My
husband's occupation was a chef in restaurants. He died from
alcoholism (September 3, 1955).*

*I know very little about the accident. When he came home
from the war he told me he killed a man in the line of duty. I
know he worried greatly over it. Everytime he became intoxicated,
he would say, 'I wish I hadn't killed that man.' I truly
think it helped to bring on his sickness. He was a very kind
man who loved everyone. These are the results of war. So many
suffer. I do not know any of the details . . ."*

*Sincerely,*

*(Mrs.) Helen S. Bell*

*es ist aus,*
that's all she wrote,
buddy . . .

## II. *Scherzo One*

come,
o mod grass-hoppers,
clad in clod-hoppers

the measure is
MEADOW
MEADOW
MEADOW
MEADOW

four,
square

meadows,
with pastures getting the measure of rivers

the measure is
FLOW-
ER
FLOW-
ER
FLOW-
ER
FLOW-
ER

a case of
four
roses,

o cloud-hoppers, clad
in wine-dark sequins—

where it ends with beer gardens
tap dancing, and prancing
small hills dancing
in dance halls

the measure is
MOUNTAIN MOUNTAIN MOUNTAIN MOUNTAIN
MOUNTAIN

"what treads within us
on that red road?"


"next moment
when I leave this room,
I shall be just as silly
as all the rest"

III. *Purgatorio*

*"The Libido is a
Dolomite;
an Eagle is an Emblem
of Desire"*

Alt-Schluderbach
bei Toblach:

in the Composing-Hut,
in the composing heat

something
"frightfully **dark**"
come in
the open
window

something "frightfully dark":

talons and pinions!

and a crow come
from under
a sofa!

suffocation:

ANGINA!
AQUILA!

"all against all"

a heart made
of red meat

a raven in
the skin

in the hut
in the art

birds
twittering

dead
birds

in
1910

IV. *Scherzo Two*

> *"if your taste has been*
> *purified in Berlin,*
> *be prepared*
> *to have it ruined"*

Dear
Pussy Gaylord,
"Possom Galore,"

Mr. Kitty,
poised

in the Showy
Daisy-Flea-Bane

(how sane, how
sanguine it all sounds)

to pounce on
chipmunks
under the porch

*Eli, Eli,*
*lama*
*sabachthani!*

"one often feels one
has got into a pub
or a sty"

the hills
around us
narrow their
yellow eyes
around us;
their claws
click into place
around us

it is a
sunny, bloody,

summer
morning

V. *Finale* (Enlargement on Lines by Joel Oppenheimer and
   Charles Olson)


against violets—
no defence!

again!
again!




who ran with summer, with
tansy




whose heart
became quiet

in the frost
of the last


chrys-
anthemum

This edition was designed, printed &
published by Cape Goliard Press Ltd.
10a Fairhazel Gardens, London N.W. 6.

Printed in Great Britain.


Photograph of Mahler, from the Mansell
Collection.
Cover & title-page illustrations by R.B. Kitaj.